VAMPIRES

Aaron Frisch

CREATIVE EDUCATION

Published by Creative Education
P.O. Box 227, Mankato, Minnesota 56002
Creative Education is an imprint of
The Creative Company
www.thecreativecompany.us

Design and production by
Christine Vanderbeek
Art direction by **Rita Marshall**
Printed in the United States of America

Photographs by Alamy (Arch White, AF
Archive, Papilio, Photos 12, Pictorial
Press Ltd), Getty Images (Ivan Bliznetsov),
iStockphoto (brentmelissa, Creativeye99,
Lise Gagne, Zacarias Pereira da Mata,
Rouzes, Jonathan Zabloski), Mary Evans
Picture Library, Shutterstock (Amy
Johansson, Mikhail), Superstock (Gary
Neil Corbett), Veer (James Griehaber,
Richard Kegler)

**Library of Congress
Cataloging-in-Publication Data**
Frisch, Aaron.
Vampires / by Aaron Frisch.
p. cm. — (That's spooky!)
Includes bibliographical references
and index.
Summary: A basic but fun exploration
of vampires—blood-sucking creatures
that can live forever—including how
they come to exist, their weaknesses, and
memorable examples from pop culture.
ISBN 978-1-60818-248-0
1. Vampires—Juvenile literature. I. Title.

GR830.V3F75 2013
398.21—dc23   2011051180

CPSIA: 070813 PO1714
9 8 7 6 5 4 3 2

CONTENTS

THAT'S SPOOKY!

IMAGINE ...

You are sleeping in an old castle on a stormy night. A bat flies into your room. Suddenly, the bat turns into a man in a black cape. He looks at your neck and shows his FANGS!

IT'S A VAMPIRE!

WHAT IS A VAMPIRE?

A vampire is a creature that drinks the blood of people. Many vampires are from a place called Transylvania. Vampires look like regular people, but they have sharper teeth.

Vampires look more normal than most monsters

BECOMING A VAMPIRE

If a vampire bites people but does not drink all their blood, those people turn into vampires, too! Or a **CURSE** might make people vampires after they die. Men, women, and even kids can become vampires.

It is not easy to stop a thirsty vampire

VAMPIRE BEHAVIOR

Vampires must drink blood to live. To do this, they usually bite people on the neck. If a vampire drinks enough blood, it can live forever! A vampire sleeps in a **COFFIN** during the day.

Vampires like to rest in coffins instead of beds

A Vampire's Powers

A vampire can turn into a bat and then fly. A vampire is strong and moves fast. It does not make a **REFLECTION** in a mirror. This lets a vampire sneak up on you!

A bat's sharp teeth look a lot like a vampire's

A Vampire's Weaknesses

Vampires stay away from **GARLIC**, holy water, and crosses. Sunlight hurts vampires, so they move around only in the dark. The only sure way to kill a vampire is by putting a **STAKE** through its heart!

Vampires hate stakes (left) and garlic (right)

FAMOUS VAMPIRES

The most famous vampire is Count
Dracula. He is a rich vampire in a book
from 1897. In the story, a vampire
hunter named Abraham Van Helsing
tries to kill Dracula.

Dracula (right) and Van Helsing (left) from movies

The *Twilight* books and movies are about vampires. But most of those vampires do not attack people. In video games like *Castlevania*, you can be a hero who fights vampires and other monsters in castles.

These are some of the vampires from *Twilight*

LAUGH LIKE A VAMPIRE

There are no such things as vampires. They exist only in stories. But it can be fun to act like a vampire. Find a black cape and fake fangs, and then laugh in a scary way. Just stay out of the sun!

A smart vampire hides his fangs before biting

LEARN TO SPOT A VAMPIRE

red eyes

pointy teeth

black cape

pale skin

leftover blood

R I.

THAT'S SPOOKY!

DICTIONARY

COFFIN a big box that dead people are buried in

CURSE a kind of magic spell that does something bad to a person

FANGS the long, pointy teeth at the front of a vampire's mouth

GARLIC a kind of plant that has a very strong smell

REFLECTION an image or picture that bounces off a mirror or window

STAKE a big piece of wood or metal that is shaped like a nail

23

THAT'S SPOOKY!

VAMPIRES

READ MORE

Besel, Jennifer M. *Vampires*. Mankato, Minn.: Capstone, 2007.

Hamilton, S. L. *Vampires*. Edina, Minn.: Abdo, 2011.

Jane, Pamela. *A Vampire Is Coming to Dinner! 10 Rules to Follow*. New York: Price Stern Sloan, 2010.

WEB SITES

ACTIVITY TV: VAMPIRE FACE PAINTING
http://www.activitytv.com/374-vampire-face-painting
This video shows you how to paint your face like a vampire.

FUNSCHOOL: HALLOWEEN
http://funschool.kaboose.com/fun-blaster/halloween/
This site has a lot of spooky games and pictures for coloring.

INDEX